Ode to Jamaica: The Land of My Birth

In the land of my birth, where the sun kisses the earth, Jamaica, the jewel, where dreams find their worth. With mountains so grand and beaches of white sand, a paradise found, a vibrant, loving land.

Reggae beats fill the air, a melody so sweet, dancing feet in the street, to the rhythmic heartbeat. The green of the hills, the blue of the sea, craft a portrait of beauty, of majesty free.

Land of wood and water, under the Caribbean sun, where the spirit of the people shines bright, never undone. From the hummingbird's flight to the pimento's spice, each corner, each sight, a treasure, a slice.

The flag flies high, black, green, and gold, A story of resilience, of courage untold. In the land of my birth, where heroes trod, we stand proud, we cherish, under the gaze of God.

Ackee and saltfish, the callaloo's embrace, a culinary journey, a unique taste. The spirit of Marley, the wisdom of Garvey, echoes of history, of a legacy hearty.

In this land of my birth, where the Dunn's River flows, the spirit of freedom, in every heart it glows. Jamaica, my island, in your embrace I'm found, in your oceans, your culture, your love knows no bound.

So here's to Jamaica, the land of my birth, a paradise on earth, of immeasurable worth. Through challenges, through triumphs, our hearts remain true, Jamaica, forever, we sing praises to you.

Jamaica's Anthem - Likkle but Wi Tallawah

In the heart of the Caribbean, where waves caress the shore, lies an island of beauty, where legends and tales soar. Jamaica, land of vibrant hues and melodies in the air, where the spirit of resilience dances everywhere.

"We're likkle but wi tallawah," echoes through the land, a mantra of strength, boldly proclaimed, hand in hand. For though our shores may be small, our spirits rise high, with determination fierce, reaching for the sky.

From the misty Blue Mountains to the sandy beaches fair, Jamaica's beauty captivates, beyond compare. In every ripple of the rivers and every sway of the palm, resides a spirit unyielding, a tranquil, yet mighty calm.

Through trials and triumphs, our history unfolds, with tales of heroes, brave and bold. Nanny of the Maroons, with courage, she led the way, Defiant against oppression, her legacy forever to stay.

In the rhythm of reggae and the pulse of the drums, lies the heartbeat of a nation, where unity becomes. From Bob Marley's lyrics to Marcus Garvey's call, Jamaica's voice resounds, standing proud and tall.

So let the world know of our resilient soul, for in our smallness, our greatness whole. "We're likkle but wi tallawah," forever we'll sing, For in the spirit of Jamaica, hope and strength ring.

Nik McKenzie

Special thanks to:

From the depths of my heart, I extend my sincerest gratitude to my cherished family. Your unwavering support and constant presence have been the bedrock of my journey.

Thank you for walking beside me, through every high and low, with love and encouragement. This adventure has been profoundly enriched by your companionship. I am endlessly grateful for your role in my life and for sharing this path with me.

Together, we've turned dreams into reality, and for that, I am forever thankful.

Nik

As you turn each page of "Colors of Jamaica: Exploring the Heartbeat of the Caribbean," you embark on a vivid journey that transcends the boundaries of imagination, inviting you to explore the soul of Jamaica without leaving your home. With every hue you add, you're not just coloring; you're traveling through the lush landscapes, historical sites, and vibrant culture that define this enchanting island.

This coloring book is your passport to Jamaica, offering a unique adventure that blends art, history, and culture into an immersive experience. As you fill the pages with color, you'll feel the warmth of the Jamaican sun, hear the rhythm of reggae music, and taste the richness of its cuisine. It's a journey that deepens your connection to Jamaica, igniting a desire to experience its beauty firsthand.

The journey through "Jamaica's Legacy" is more than an artistic endeavor; it's a call to explore, to learn, and to embrace the vibrant spirit of Jamaica. And who knows? Perhaps this coloring book will inspire your next adventure, leading you to walk the sandy beaches, climb the majestic Blue Mountains, and dance to the beat of reggae in the land where this music was born.

So, let "Colors of Jamaica: Exploring the Heartbeat of the Caribbean" be the start of your journey to Jamaica, where each page turned is a step closer to the heart of this beautiful island. And remember, the true essence of Jamaica awaits not just in the colors you choose but in the adventures you'll embark upon, inspired by the stories and landscapes you've brought to life through your creativity.

JAMAICA
FEEL THE HEART
AND SOUL OF A NATION

Jamaica - A Tapestry of History and Heritage

Jamaica, an island nation situated in the Caribbean Sea, is renowned for its vibrant culture, stunning natural beauty, and significant historical contributions. Here's an overview of its history, notable heroes, and key resources:

History:

Indigenous Inhabitants: Prior to European colonization, Jamaica was inhabited by the Taíno people, who called the island "Xaymaca," meaning "land of wood and water."

Spanish Colonization: Christopher Columbus arrived in Jamaica in 1494 during his second voyage to the Americas. The Spanish colonized the island in the early 16th century, bringing African slaves to work on plantations.

British Rule: In 1655, the British seized control of Jamaica from the Spanish. The island became a British colony, and the sugar industry flourished with the use of slave labor.

Emancipation and Independence: Slavery was abolished in 1834, leading to significant social and economic changes. Jamaica gained independence from British rule on August 6, 1962, becoming a sovereign nation within the Commonwealth.

The Maroons: Descendants of escaped African slaves who formed independent communities in Jamaica's mountainous interior, played a significant role in the island's history. These communities, known as Maroon settlements, were established during the period of British colonization when slaves fled from plantations seeking freedom and autonomy.

One of the most notable Maroon leaders was Queen Nanny, who led the Windward Maroons in fierce resistance against British forces in the early 18th century. Nanny's strategic brilliance and her community's knowledge of the terrain enabled them to successfully defend their territory and maintain their freedom.

The Maroons often engaged in guerrilla warfare tactics, utilizing their intimate knowledge of the Jamaican landscape to outmaneuver British troops. Through treaties and agreements, the Maroons eventually secured semi-autonomous status, allowing them to govern their own communities and preserve their cultural traditions.

Today, the Maroon communities in Jamaica, such as Accompong and Moore Town, continue to uphold their unique cultural practices, including traditional music, dance, and spirituality. They are celebrated as symbols of resistance, resilience, and the enduring legacy of Jamaica's fight for freedom.

Modern Era: Since independence, Jamaica has experienced periods of political and economic challenges but has also made significant strides in areas such as education, sports, and culture.

Jamaica - A Tapestry of History and Heritage

Notable Heroes:

Marcus Garvey: A prominent Jamaican political leader, publisher, journalist, and orator, Garvey was a key figure in the Pan-Africanism movement, advocating for the unity and empowerment of African descendants worldwide.

Nanny of the Maroons: Nanny, a legendary Maroon leader, played a crucial role in Jamaica's resistance against British colonization in the 18th century. She is revered as a symbol of strength, resilience, and freedom.

Bob Marley: Reggae music icon Bob Marley is perhaps Jamaica's most globally recognized figure. His music, infused with messages of social justice and spirituality, continues to inspire people around the world.

Resources:

Tourism: Jamaica's stunning beaches, lush mountains, and rich cultural heritage make it a popular tourist destination. Tourism is a significant contributor to the country's economy, providing employment opportunities and foreign exchange earnings.

Bauxite: Jamaica possesses large deposits of bauxite, the primary use is in aluminum production. Bauxite mining has been a major industry in Jamaica, contributing to economic development but also raising environmental concerns.

Agriculture: Agriculture remains an important sector in Jamaica, with crops such as sugarcane, bananas, coffee, and citrus fruits being cultivated. The island's fertile soil and tropical climate support diverse agricultural activities.

Blue Mountain Coffee: Jamaica's Blue Mountain coffee is renowned worldwide for its exceptional quality and flavor. Grown in the misty Blue Mountains, this coffee variety is highly sought after and commands premium prices in international markets.

Jamaica's history, heroes, and resources collectively reflect the island's rich heritage, resilience, and contributions to the global community.

Landmarks and Historical Sites

Dunns River Falls

Dunns River Falls

Port Royal

Port Royal

Rose Hall Great House

Rose Hall Great House

Flora and Fauna

Jamaican Humming Bird (Doctor Bird)

Jamaican Humming Bird (Doctor Bird)

Jamaican Humming Bird (Doctor Bird)

Blue and John Crow Mountains National Park

Blue and John Crow Mountains National Park

Blue and John Crow Mountains National Park

Culture and People

Reggae Music

Reggae Music

Market Scene

Market Scene

Traditonal Dress and Festivals

Traditonal Dress and Festivals

Beach and Coastal Life

Seven Mile Beach

Seven Mile Beach

Seven Mile Beach

Negril Lighthouse and Coastal View

Negril Lighthouse and Coastal View

Negril Lighthouse and Coastal View

Jamaican Cuisine

Fruits and Spice

Fruits and Spice

Traditional Dish - Jerk Chicken

Jack Fruit

Ackee

**Sugar Cane

Jamaican Patios Phases

WAH GWAAN?

What's going on? How are you

Jamaican Patios

MI SOON COME

I'll be right back

Jamaican Patios

TEK IT EASY

Take it easy

Jamaican Patios

NUH WORRY YUHSELF

Don't worry about it

Jamaican Patios

ONE LOVE

A term of endearment and a
universal greeting

Popularized by Bob Marley

Flag and Map of Jamaica

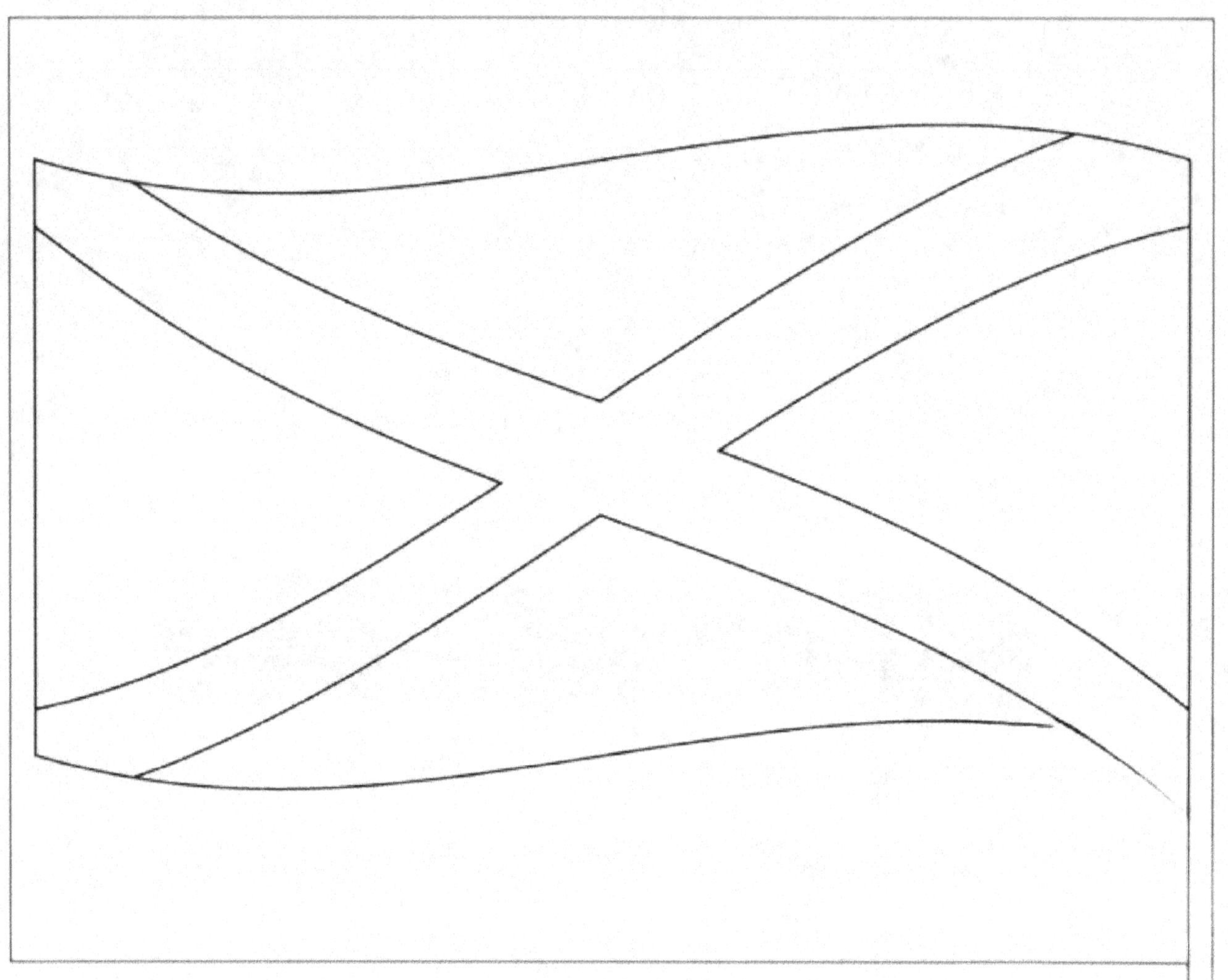

Symbolism of the Jamaican flag

The Jamaican flag's meaning can be interpreted concisely and poetically as:
"The sun shineth, the land is green, and the people are strong and creative."
In other words, the colors of the Jamaican flag stand for the sun (gold), the land
(green), and the people (black)

FLORIDA
Atlantic Ocean
BAHAMAS
CUBA
JAMAICA
Kingston
HAITI
DOMINICAN REPUBLIC
Caribbean Sea

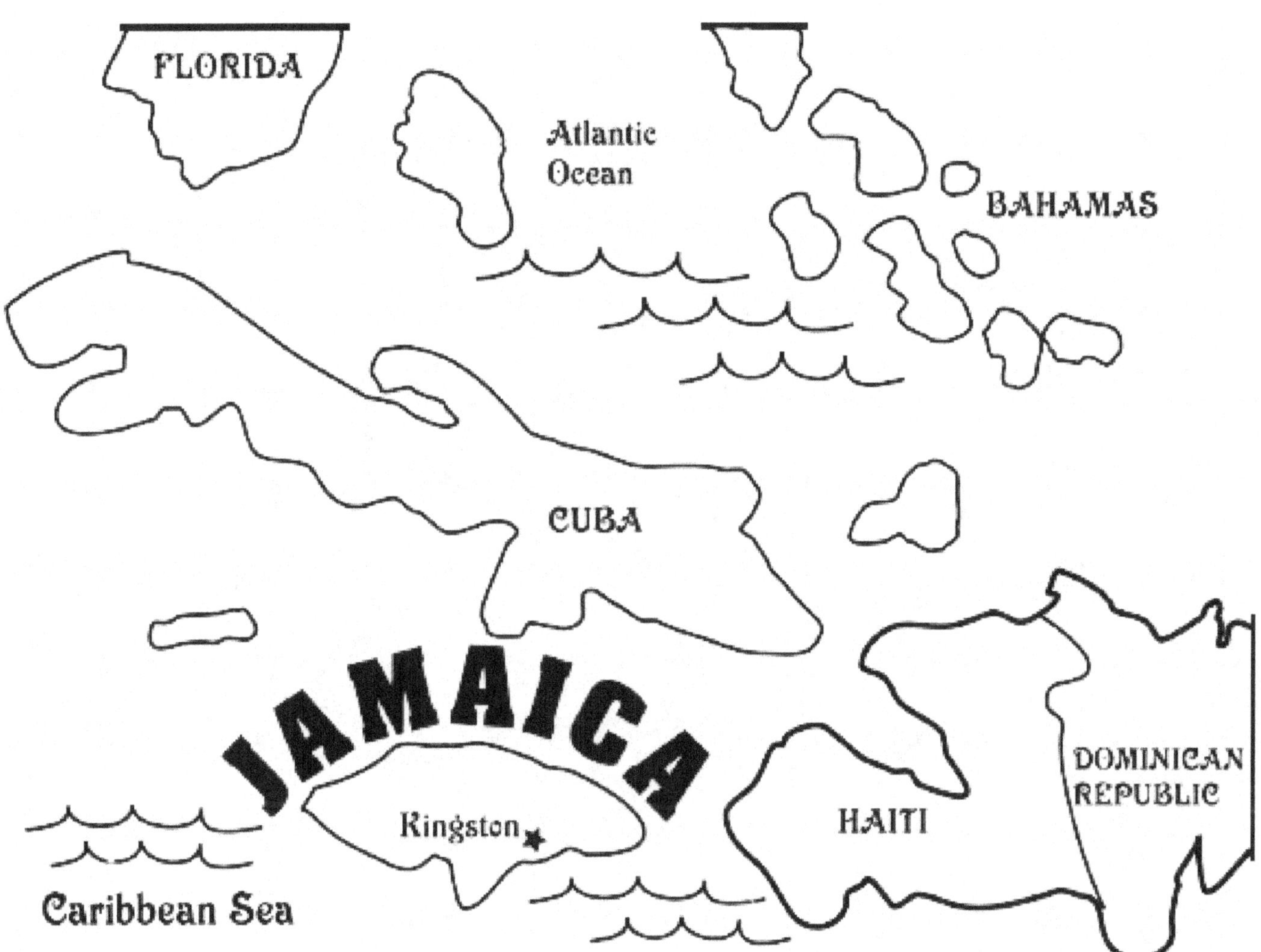

Jamaica

Jamaica Map Outline

Jamaica

JAMAICA

```
D  N  A  L  S  I  F  L  O  U  Q  R  Z  E  T
Z  K  A  W  E  A  T  L  O  E  Z  W  I  B  F
G  K  K  Q  M  I  S  A  B  A  T  R  H  Q  K
S  D  Z  B  R  Z  L  H  M  G  I  W  O  I  M
M  A  R  L  E  Y  T  E  A  G  M  A  N  G  O
A  O  O  D  Y  A  S  C  B  E  F  G  U  T  N
J  L  A  V  I  B  I  N  U  R  S  X  C  N  T
E  H  T  N  E  P  O  A  R  T  V  R  Y  R  E
R  U  O  E  K  T  T  D  O  E  A  L  S  K  G
K  M  K  B  K  T  A  N  C  S  E  B  U  K  O
M  C  H  L  E  C  P  T  I  O  L  F  N  Q  E
A  K  A  U  X  A  I  A  M  U  R  E  P  G  D
E  E  F  F  O  C  C  R  B  H  P  A  U  B  C
T  U  R  T  L  E  B  H  C  O  R  K  L  L  Z
C  A  R  N  I  V  A  L  Q  U  G  Y  B  P  B
```

Find the word in the puzzle.

Words can go in any direction.
Words can share letters as they cross over each other.

Ackee	Bamboo	Beach
Blue	Carnival	Coffee
Coral	Cricket	Dancehall
Irie	Island	Jerk
Kingston	Mango	Marley
Montego	Patois	Rasta
Reef	Reggae	Rum
Ska	Sun	Taino
Turtle		

Marcus Garvey 

Marcus Garvey was a seminal figure in the history of the African diaspora, an inspirational leader whose ideas and actions have left a lasting impact on the fight for racial equality and the promotion of African heritage. Here are key facts about Marcus Garvey:

Early Life: Marcus Mosiah Garvey Jr. was born on August 17, 1887, in St. Ann's Bay, Jamaica. He was the youngest of 11 children, only two of whom survived to adulthood.

Education and Early Career: Garvey was largely self-educated. He worked as a printer and newspaper editor in Jamaica, where he began to develop his political views and advocate for workers' rights.

Universal Negro Improvement Association (UNIA): In 1914, Garvey founded the UNIA in Jamaica, aiming to promote African Americans' return to Africa, their ancestral homeland, and to foster a global economic independence and strong sense of black pride and unity. The UNIA grew to become the largest African-American organization.

Move to the United States: Garvey moved to Harlem, New York, in 1916, where he re-established the UNIA and began publishing the Negro World newspaper, promoting his ideas of black nationalism and pan-Africanism.

Black Star Line: In 1919, Garvey established the Black Star Line, a shipping line intended to facilitate the transportation of goods and eventually African Americans throughout the African global economy. The venture aimed to connect the black communities across the Americas, Caribbean, and Africa.

Back-to-Africa Movement: Garvey was a leading advocate of the Back-to-Africa movement, which encouraged those of African descent to return to the African countries of their ancestors. This was part of his broader vision of an independent black nation.

Legal Troubles and Deportation: In 1923, Garvey was convicted in the United States for mail fraud in connection with the Black Star Line. Many historians and supporters believe the charges were politically motivated to undermine his influence. He was imprisoned in 1925 and later deported to Jamaica in 1927.

Later Years and Legacy: After his deportation, Garvey continued his activism in Jamaica and then moved to London in 1935, where he lived until his death in 1940. Garvey's legacy is a lasting influence on future civil rights movements, and he is seen as a forefather of the Rastafari movement, pan-Africanism, and Black Pride movements.

Philosophy and Influence: Garvey's philosophy, often summarized by the phrases "Africa for Africans" and "One God, One Aim, One Destiny," continues to inspire and influence a wide range of movements and individuals around the world, including the Nation of Islam and the Civil Rights Movement in the United States.

Marcus Garvey's vision of empowering black people and his relentless pursuit of equality and justice have cemented his place as one of the most influential black leaders in history.

Ms. Lou (Louise Bennett-Coverley)

Louise Bennett-Coverley, affectionately known as Miss Lou, was a beloved Jamaican poet, folklorist, writer, and educator. Born on September 7, 1919, in Kingston, Jamaica, she became one of the most influential figures in Jamaican literature and culture. Here are key facts about Miss Lou:

Early Life and Education: Louise Bennett was born in Kingston, Jamaica, and was educated at Excelsior High School in Kingston. She later studied at the Royal Academy of Dramatic Art in London, England, where she honed her skills in drama and performance.

Cultural Ambassador: Miss Lou is renowned for her commitment to preserving Jamaican Patois (Creole), the language spoken by the majority of Jamaicans. At a time when the use of Patois was stigmatized, she celebrated it in her poetry and performances, helping to elevate its status and promote Jamaican cultural identity.

Contributions to Jamaican Culture: Through her poems, performances, and radio broadcasts, Miss Lou played a pivotal role in promoting Jamaican folklore, traditions, and language. She was a pioneer in using Jamaican Patois in literature, breaking down social barriers and fostering a sense of pride in Jamaican heritage.

Legacy and Honors: Miss Lou's contributions to Jamaican culture were widely recognized. She received numerous awards and honors, including the Order of Jamaica (1974) and the Order of Merit (2001), the country's third-highest honor. Her legacy continues to influence Jamaican culture, education, and the arts.

Notable Works: Miss Lou wrote several collections of poetry that include iconic pieces celebrating Jamaican life, culture, and language. Two of her most famous poems are:

"Colonization in Reverse": This poem humorously comments on the migration of Jamaicans to England, highlighting the cultural impact Jamaicans had in the UK.

"No Lickle Twang": This poem playfully addresses the issue of language and identity, emphasizing pride in the Jamaican dialect over adopting a foreign accent.

Miss Lou's dedication to Jamaican Patois and her efforts to celebrate and legitimize the language have left an indelible mark on the cultural landscape of Jamaica.

Quiz Time

1. **When was Marcus Garvey born?** _______________________________________

2. **What is Marcus Garvey known for?**_______________________________________

3. **What was Marcus Garvey's main teachings?**_______________________________

4. **What was Marcus Garvey convicted of ?**_________________________________

1. **When was Ms. Lou born?** _______________________________________

2. **What is Ms. Lou known for?**_______________________________________

3. **What did Ms. Lou contribute to Jamaica?**_______________________________

4. **Name one of Ms. Lou's poem?**_________________________________

All about Jamaica Quiz

1. How many parishes does Jamaica? ____

2. What year did Jamaica gain independence?____

3. Name a notable hero other than Marcis Garvey and Ms. Lou ? ___________________

4. What is bauxite used for ?____

5. Where is blue moutain coffee grown?____

6. What decendants of escaped African slaves formed an independent community in

   Jamaica? ____

7. What is the motto of Jamaica?____

As you color the final page of "Colors of Jamaica: Exploring the Heartbeat of the Caribbean," you find yourself at the end of a remarkable journey through the heart of Jamaica. With each stroke of color, you've traversed the vibrant streets, lush landscapes, and rich history that make this island uniquely captivating. This coloring book has been more than a collection of illustrations; it has been a gateway to experiencing Jamaica's soul, its people, and its culture.

Now, standing at the threshold of this artistic voyage, you carry with you a deeper appreciation for the island's beauty and heritage. The colors you've chosen and the scenes you've brought to life have woven a personal connection to Jamaica, inviting you to explore its reality beyond the pages.

This isn't just the end of a coloring book; it's the beginning of a journey. Inspired by the images you've colored and the stories they tell, you may find yourself dreaming of walking along the sandy shores of Negril, feeling the mist from Dunn's River Falls on your skin, or swaying to the rhythms of reggae music under a starlit sky.

"Colors of Jamaica: Exploring the Heartbeat of the Caribbean" has offered you a glimpse into the island's soul, but the true adventure begins with stepping onto its land, breathing its air, and immersing yourself in the vibrant culture you've only just begun to explore. Until that day comes, let the pages you've colored serve as a reminder of the beauty, resilience, and spirit of Jamaica, calling you to one day experience its wonders in person.

May the journey you've embarked upon through this coloring book inspire you to explore further, to learn more, and to one day find yourself on the shores of Jamaica, where the colors of your imagination meet the reality of its endless beauty.

Quiz Answers

Marcus Garvey

1. August 17, 1887
2. Empowering black people and his relentless pursuit of equality and justice
3. Civil Rights
4. Mail Fraud in 1923

Ms. Lou

1. September 7, 1919
2. Commitment to preserving Jamaican Patois
3. She played a pivotal role in promoting Jamaican folklore, traditions, and language
4. "No Lickle Twang"

All about Jamaica Quiz

1. 14 parishes
2. August 6, 1962
3. Nanny, a legendary Maroon leader
4. Aluminum production
5. The Maroon's
6. Jamaica's Anthem - Likkle but Wi Tallawah